Convalescence: An anthology of poetry

Allison Carroll

BookLeaf Publishing

Presentation by *BookLeaf Publishing*

Web: www.bookleafpub.com

E-mail: info@bookleafpub.com

ISBN: 9789357445771

First edition 2022

DEDICATION

For Nan, who taught me to laugh at myself.

And for Mike, who taught me to drive, to swim, and to fly.

ACKNOWLEDGEMENTS

I'd like to thank my partner Matt for, once again, putting up with my mania, and for always being the biggest supporter of both my work and my wellness.

I'd also like to thank my talented pal Tonia M'igyver (T. Doe) for giving permission to use her work (titled "Alien") on the book's cover. I am the proud owner of the original painting, which hangs in splendour on the wall in my office.

Try Again

I wake in the heavy afternoon air
trapped under the heft of the duvet.
How is it I feel nothing useful,
and yet everything else?

Today I'll try driving again,
though I have no sense about me:
no wisdom, no art, no ambition.
I always thought I was dumb.

Always the last sitting
in cavernous exam halls
with their stifling, boggy air,
forever ravenous for more time.

My brain could never unstop itself
satisfactorily, as if from
a measured bottle; I could make do
though never very well.

I grow older and everything
is a little bit more unbearable
and unyielding, like an iron poker
stoking a hot coal fire.

One year since you left,
a month since letting go,
six weeks since the break, and
day one of quitting the bed.

Unlucky Alchemy

the rainbow is still painted there
on the window of the front room
some oil, water, and coloured dye, while
another body fills your tomb

it makes me just furious
but then, what exactly are we?
carbon, hydrogen, calcium, nitrogen
suspended in lucky alchemy

how many times have I sat here
in this very same spot
white lines on tarmac
while I feel myself rot

the sun touched us equally
this June and the last
but I fill space, useless
as you meet your untimely rest

Home Away From Home

home away from home
museum of happier times
it snatches my breath from me
soon as I walk inside

yours was the house
always kept so cold,
you, the parents who'd soothe
and never really scold

where now do I run
broken-limbed, broken-hearted
when the missing of you cripples me
the longer we are parted?

In the Dark, Unbelonging

Duty, as bold as brass
brought me to this space,
while obligation was an acid
I'd swallow whenever it came
up with my speech.
But still, I wore these burdens well
as if pinned to my lapel
for every passing person to see.

I once belonged here,
papers and records told me so
Beryl and Norma, too --
the latter in her pastel frock
selling sweets to residents,
gifting them with her smiles,
and teaching me how
to make change.

This temporary internment
is stretching out into a season.
With no grave to hold you,

I come here without reason.
With shaky hands on the wheel
I sit in the dark, unbelonging,
waiting for the rest of this
loathsome world to wake.

I Can't Be Well

I get up, and
every day I show up.
Sometimes I feed myself.
Sometimes, instead, I'm fed up,
but I swear that I
get it right most times.

The last time I wore these clothes
they were still alive, and
since then nothing hangs right.
His breaths were stolen,
she forgot her music,
and I lie awake half the night.

I'm livid with the sunset
while they're not here to see it.
It has no business
being at all beautiful
and I'm always taking it
personally.

Please, just give me this
I have my whole life to learn
how to be well, but now

I must be hollow; I’m fucking busy
burying this black grief
six inches deep.

The World Forgot Me

I went out into the world today
hesitant and bashful,
as if the world forgot me,
having not seen my face
unburdened and uncovered
from the shields I carry:
some gilded, some silken
equally as potent.

I paid someone else to brew my coffee, asked
that it be made delicate and sweet, then put all
the windows down,
letting the breeze move languidly
across my face and put its fingers
into my tangled hair --
the first touch I felt
outside my home in weeks.

Do not tell me this isn't real;
I know it is, as sure as my
blood churns and gurgles,

throbbing down derma highways,
oiling my stiffened limbs and
inciting them to move.
This great beast is awakening,
clinging fast to its mortal coil.

A Year In Red

I received the shoes today
made of gathered lace
and inlaid with spangling gems,
incongruous pearls -- all false,
but you could never tell.

I slip them on and
will myself to move a little,
gliding across the filthy rug
and taking the greatest care
not to stumble.

I needn't have bothered.
Six seasons have turned over
and I finally feel ready, but
no matter; I lift my pen
and mark the next year in red.

It Didn't Matter

I broke a limb and
willed it to mend.
I still feel some pain but
it's already moving again.
It didn't really matter.

I broke a promise,
broke another, and then
forgiveness was given.
I was a bad friend, but
now it doesn't matter.

My heart was sundered:
I lost nearly all my kin.
Some got well, some didn't,
it's marked on their skin.
None of it will matter.

We watched, did not impeach,
but applauded the keynote speech.
We failed in our outreach, and
recalled the book meant to teach
us but, would it even have mattered?

I created art, made meals of medicine,
watered myself but remained unquenched,
exercised my body and my mouth, and
I even climbed mountains, but
I'm waiting for it to matter.

The Light's Still On

I go to your empty house
and out of lingering respect,
take my shoes off
at the door like always,
though no one here
would mind the dirt
I'm tracking in.
Everything is unmoved;
it even smells the same,
and I know now your activities
were never its true source.
It seems this good house
has a life of its own.
I can hear the grates sighing,
and the worn floorboards creak
of their own accord now.
The light's on a timer -
it flickers on unknowingly,
lighting a beacon through the curtains
to help bring you home.
It hasn't given up yet,
but soon, it will likely dim
the way all things do
after too much time.

I pour a lukewarm Pepsi
into a dusty glass with
my capable hands, and
sit down on the couch
(I'm sure it's still allowed),
and even throw a blanket
over my cold feet –
I'm certain it's glad
to be of use again.
The television still jumps,
flickering into life,
and, resentful, I flip
through the news,
the TV guide, and
watch snippets of shows
that always made you laugh
(but you were always gracious
with your laughter), and
I'm content again
for a little while
until the knowing
noiselessly presses in.

Prufrocking

Through the twittering crowd
I see familiar fragments and know them all:
too-tight blouses, blazers woven with mould,
the dimly-lit table lamps glowing
in a hazy, perfumed fog
of stale breath and potpourri.
People mill about, heels sinking
into the dense, stain-laden carpet
and soon I'm thinking about
the grim humanity of it all.
We are large vials of juices
suspended in sagging skin,
sloshing around, liable to spill
in a single moment of crisis.
The mighty Davids will fall,
succumb to their Goliaths,
limbs jutting out like shards of glass
causing the rest to recoil
and keep a safe distance.
We shuffle in a circular motion,
an intimate machine of evasion
forever moving, yet never forward.
I watch those who break off
from this conga danse macabre

and make their way through the gloom,
their pulsing blood causing them to dare.

The Immediacy of Things

I can dream up so many faces
that I would like to see
in the waking hours,
while seeking the flight patterns
of iridescent and errant birds,
and noticing the worn trails
of insects busying themselves
on the petals of flowers
planted in remembrance.

I feel desperately lost
until nature reminds me
of the immediacy of things:
food to be buried,
and young to be born,
while striving not to be seen;
burrows to dig,
tracks to cover,
and wounds to be licked clean.

The Deed

It spreads like a virus from
the center of the diamond,
the anvil that anchors the band,
then seeps down the finger,
and the veined highways
to the head and heart.

It slithers into the mouth and
coils up, waiting to leap out
when you recite your new name.
It slides along the tiled floor
of the bank with ease, worms its way
into your vault, and then feasts.

It wraps around your body
and fastens you in your place.
It holds you down on the bed,
beneath the highest rank,
or at arm's length of the
austere and gilded throne.

I'll not be sold or owned,
or allow the shackling of my soul.
There'll be no false identity

tacked to the end of my name
like Luther's ninety-five theses,
proclaiming what to change.

Jane Doe

More lifelike near death,
face flushed with the colour red
spilling in rivers from her mouth, nostrils
and the temples of her head.
And she's black on the inside –
you shoved your disease into her
over and over, as if you
were serving on a chain gang,
rocking her body back and forth
like a mop used to clean a dirty floor.
Then she'd marinate in the hate
you also splashed across her face:
a shining target, a mirror reflection
that you hit and clawed at
like a rabid animal, until
you no longer recognized yourself.
Dragged by skirt or ponytail
you painted her luscious purples and blues,
until like a wilted pansy, she drooped,
and you could avoid all the blame.
They all side with you,
the faceless football players,
while a sleepless, faceless girl
somewhere forgets her name.

Convalescing

The doctors I see are in league
with a body that's gotten
completely away from me.
Until now it's been so easy
to ignore a racing mind,
and a rapidly beating heart
grown many sizes too big.
They try to tell me
this is exactly the time
for silence, for brooding,
for sitting still and
steeping in my sorrow,
and they call it convalescing.
Don't they know
that I've laid low
for far too long?
If I have to stew here,
I'm doing it my way.
If those I loved aren't somewhere
as good as how they lived,
I reserve the right to riot,
to drive straight through
the stolid hospital wing, to
kick every shingle off its roof,

and maybe then I'll feel
relief at proper consequences.
I don't want to depend on the bliss
caused by those paid to care for me.
I won't wallow, or pickle in this brine --
I have a little pride.
Pay me what I'm worth,
and I'll only stay longer,
and spend every dollar
on a wedding to myself,
and I'll do it when
I'm good and ready.

I'm Always Losing

I lost a job, and then another –
no fault of my own, or so it's been said
but this syndrome gives me doubt, and
stops me from living outside my head.

It's never not condescending
to ask if I can care for myself,
but if I'm honest, I struggle
to remember the bottle on the shelf.

Like some of Bishop's Arts,
I'm losing so many things,
while past disasters loom, and
predict what the future brings.

How does it feel to me?
My body keeps the score,
and I'm no better off
than I ever was before.

The Waves of Southampton

On the banks of Lake Huron
where all the children play
at being kings and queens,
lies a town of mostly retirees
that I would have overlooked
if not for the love that brought me.

I allow the sun to warm
and the sand to bury, and know
when I let myself go to seed,
that the waves of Southampton
will beat me back and bear me
always in the way that I need.

An Accident

The way time makes its choices
I'll never understand:
its victims and its survivors,
what causes it to bend, or
to do the Devil's deeds.

Outcomes change in mere seconds,
speeding forward or out of the way.
You can open the jaws of life,
and regurgitate second chances,
granting space for some recovery.

I'll always urge aluminum,
steel, fire, and glass
to forge, rather than break
bridges across a dark impasse,
(just in case they have any say).

Life’s Teachings

In the landscape of this empty year
old teachers have re-entered my life,
and I’m left wondering why.
I’m always grasping, reaching
for some greater meaning
to prove I’m worth something
beyond just idle praise.
Maybe they’ve come back
to guide me once again.
I’m forever filled with questions
that need immediate answers.
Was it all some great exchange?
Did the others go, so my Mother could stay?
My joy is forever tinged.
Of all the things I’ve learned,
the only thing that’s stayed
is that it does no harm
to cure someone of simple doubts.
So why can’t it be done for me?
Life moves ever circularly.

Undue Labour

Tax-paying, law-abiding,
I feel like I'm good inside,
apart from being breakable
and my agency being denied.

Food is plucked from my fingertips
and my doctor says I'm too fat.
I must learn to sustain myself,
but apparently not like that.

It's laughable that you expect me
to give a single shit about my recovery
when I'm taught to devalue myself
and subsist on less than I need.

When I'm denied that which is owed
for grief unprocessed, and labour unpaid
when even my therapist forgets me,
the cost is simply too great.

Writing Just To Say

I cannot write a poem today.
The day is just too short,
and the air is way too hot.
I can't give space to this pain
every single day.

My arm is as broken
as my spirit these days,
so I'm just writing this to say
that I can't wait to be
the aunt you were to me.

This Starving Season

This starving season
I am moved to redecorate
the dank walls of my mind
using discarded paint swatches
from attempted restorations past
and detritus littering the floor.
I need something softer this time
unassuming turquoise, bodied creams,
colours that are earthen
and can be found in nature,
which constantly surprises me,
but never enough to
lead me to delight, into believing
in gods, or the Words Worth
something still, locked away
in my tower of uni textbooks
holding up these broken beams.
I'll rid myself of those burdens, too
and consider adding some other hues:
blushing Ontario peach, honeyed yellows
to remind me of the breakfasts

brought to me at noon hour
when I am still in bed, and
when the blinds are opened
to let the light rush in.
With these tastes under my tongue
I choose to close out my fears
as they circle me like birds
in this oppressive attic air.
I shoo them into nonexistence, and
replace them with the greenest vines
hung like party streamers,
and intricate shapes done in macramé.
I am doing a thorough housekeeping here.
I drape velvet over the mould,
hang art over the holes, and
fill every crack with
the very best of intentions.
I feed fairy lights through the cobwebs
and excite the dust,
waking this sturdy structure
while shouting all down the halls
in a voice loud enough to carry
out the open window and down the block:
someone lives here.

www.ingramcontent.com/pod-product-compliance
Lightning Source LLC
Chambersburg PA
CBHW051748130826
49812CB00033B/1051
9789357445771